Before you read this book,
please think about the following questions:

Do you know what makes a good citizen?
Could you list five qualities of a good citizen?

Take a moment to discuss the answers.
Now see if those qualities are inside!

The ABCs of How to Be a Good Citizen
Copyright © 2019 by Marybeth Zuhlke

ISBN 13: 978-1-73233-361-1
ISBN 10: 1-73233-361-0

Library of Congress PCN 2019934413

To order a copy of this book, please contact
AMITY Publications
www.amitypublications.com

Printed in the United States of America

The ABCs of
How to Be a Good Citizen

To Juliette ~ an outstanding citizen and friend!

Marybeth Zuhlke

Written by Marybeth Zuhlke
Illustrated by Diana Raucina

A

Act responsibly.

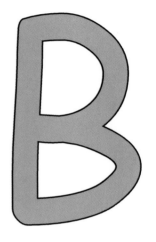

Be courteous.

C

Create positive relationships.

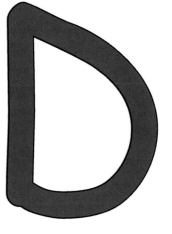

Do good things like volunteer.

E

Enjoy and respect the environment.

F

Forgive and forget.

Get to work and set goals.

Help others whenever you can.

I

Interact with people of all nationalities.

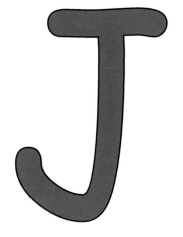

Join clubs like
Girl Scouts and Boy Scouts.

K

Know your country and its laws.

Things I'm thankful for

- Family
- Friends
- Home
- Food
- School
- Holidays
- Etc.

L

List things you are grateful for.

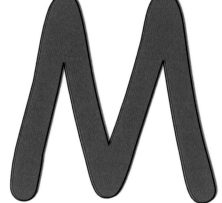

Motivate yourself to read books.

Never give up.

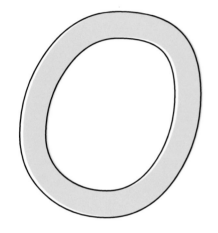

Open your mind
to all points of view.

Practice peace and love.

**Quietly listen
when someone is talking.**

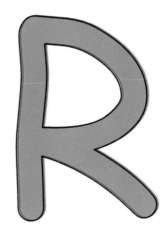

Respect other people's opinions.

Stand up for your beliefs.

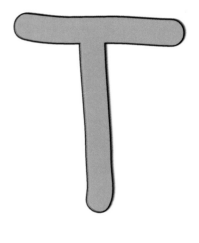

Treat all living things kindly.

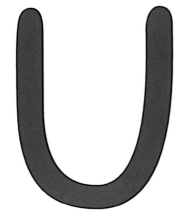

Understand each other's feelings.

Vote!

W

Watch the news and be informed.

eXamine your values and
set a good example.

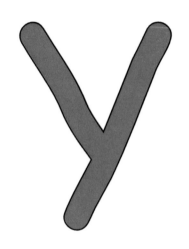

You can do it if
you put your mind to it.

Zoom in and remember
the rights of all citizens.

REFLECT PEACE

Practice polite behavior.
Encourage and help each other.
Accept each person for who they are.
Create a caring atmosphere.
Enjoy and respect the environment.

THE BIG THREE RULES

Always be courteous.

Think before you act.

Delay gratification.

<u>NO ACT OF KINDNESS IS EVER WASTED.</u>

Here's some ideas to help spread kindness:

Write someone a kind note.
Give a teacher a compliment.
Smile at someone today.
Tell a parent they are doing a good job.
Say hi to someone you don't know.
Ask your teacher if they need some help.
Tell someone you are happy to see them.
Read a book to a younger child.
Invite someone to sit with you at lunch.

My name is Marybeth Safransky VanLanduyt Zuhlke. I was an elementary teacher in Kenosha Unified Schools for many years. I am one of the Co-Founders of Peace Learning Circles. The idea for this book began 20 years ago while teaching third grade. I often brainstormed with the students using the ABC' as a way to motivate them to learn new words by playing "Dictionary Dig." Students would use a paperback dictionary, call out a letter and then find a word that would fit the theme of the book we were writing. One of my students chose the letter "I" and wrote: "I have good ideas on how to be a good citizen" and that's how the first "ABCs of How to Be a Good Citizen" was born.

The letters of the alphabet have been a cornerstone of all my teaching. They reflect my philosophy of education - Always be Courteous, Always be Caring, and Always be Curious. I have supervised student teachers for the University of Wisconsin – Parkside and encourage them to use the ABC technique. I have worked with middle school students at John XXIII Education Center in Racine, WI, using the ABC technique, to teach citizenship. Some of their ideas have been incorporated into this book.

In 2017, I attended a Character Education Conference at Alverno College, Milwaukee, Wisconsin. The True Colors of Character was the theme. It was then I decided to update and publish "The ABCs of How to Be a Good Citizen." Hopefully, when you read it, you will think of more ways to be a good citizen and practice peace. Together, we can build a better world.

My name is Diana Vinogradova Raucina. I am an artist at heart. I was born in Latvia, a Baltic country in Eastern Europe. I attended Art School of Jurmala, Latvia for four years. I earned a college degree in architecture, graduating in 2015 from Riga Building College in Latvia. I moved to Kenosha, Wisconsin after my marriage to Drew Raucina.

Since I was a child, I have been drawing, painting, and making various art designs. I love to create canvas paintings, postcards, 3D models, and hand drawn sketches.

I am now a Facilitator for Peace Learning Circles workshops for elementary and middle schools in southeastern Wisconsin. We work to help children understand and respect people of all cultures and encourage them to become better citizens and peacemakers.

Read what people are saying about this book!

"A "must" tool in aiding young minds in this country. In fact, every country will benefit from its simple and inspiring approach." - *Nabeeh El-Amin, Racine Islamic Center*

"The book "The ABCs of How to Be a Good Citizen" is an excellent resource for a beginning teacher and someone new to the American Education system. I value the information in this book." - *Xue Qing Jiang/Ginger Price*

"An excellent primer to bring our youth to a profound understanding of their responsibility and American Citizenship." - *Bob Iglar, Retired Accountant*

"This is an awesome book. I love each message for the letters. Great messages for kids to follow and parents to read with them." - *April Harris, Parent*

"In today's society, teaching manners, kindness and citizenship are current topics. As these can be challenging to re-direct children's actions, this book does it in a kid-friendly manner. Please read it aloud with your child and discuss each page." - *Sandra Steeves, School Librarian*

"My favorite letter is "U" - Understand each other's feelings. If we try to understand each other's feelings, we will all get along better." - *Jermarius Harris, 6th grade, 21st Century Prep School*

"Stewardship is an integral part of being a good citizen. Taking care of Mother Earth is also mandatory for all good citizens. This book exemplifies all the words we need to live by." - *Vittoria Du Mez, Actress and Entertainer*

"This ABC book is very accessible to young children and the layout of the color art work on the pages catches the eye as well as the heart. The message in word and illustration is clear and important in our world today." - *Denise Zingg, Director of Spectrum School of Art, Racine, WI*

"As a colleague of Marybeth for many years, I have witnessed first-hand the motivational aspects of her ABC book. The updated, beautifully illustrated new version is easy to understand and apply. It provides a springboard to discussion and positive action while building a foundation of good citizenship." - *Ann Wojciechowicz, retired 3rd grade teacher*

"Congratulations to Marybeth and Diana for recognizing the importance of teaching good citizenship to children when they are young. The world would be a better place if these ABCs were adopted." - *Esther Letven, Retired Asst. Chancellor, UW-Parkside*

"This ABC Book relates totally to the 2nd grade curriculum. We cover citizenship! I enjoy how every letter of the alphabet is illustrated in a "positive" way!" - *Anna Eckelberg, Grade 2 Teacher , KTEC East, Kenosha, WI*

Peace Learning Circles

In 2005, Peace Learning Circles was established in Kenosha and Racine, WI by Juliette Garesche, Sue Hollow, Denis Wikel, and Marybeth Zuhlke.

PLC is a program that helps students and community members to be more peaceful and to develop good citizenship. The mission promotes a culture of peace through education to youth and communities. The vision is that our homes, schools, and place of work, worship and play will be a welcoming and safe place where everyone is included, respected, and cherished. The goal is that people will join together to make communities a safer place to live, emotionally, physically, and mindfully. To do this we must have two things - knowledge and willingness.

Peace Mentors we aspire to be like...

**Dr. Martin Luther King, Jr.   ~   Mother Teresa
Mahatma Gandhi   ~   Cesar Chavez   ~   Malala Yousafzai**

For more information, visit www.peacelearningcircles.org.

"We teach our students to be good citizens, good classmates, good brothers and sisters, and good sons and daughters. We work from inside out, building stronger students on the inside so that they can be kinder and more helpful to others on the outside. We teach our students strategies to practice peace, to prevent bullying, to resolve conflicts peacefully, and to be ambassadors of peace. We teach our students how to be team builders and how to include everyone in the classroom and on the playground. Our goal is to develop student leaders who work together to create a kinder, more compassionate school learning environment."

Joe Mangi
PLC Board President
Former Superintendent and Principal

Made in the USA
Lexington, KY
19 December 2019